Economic Depression

What It Is and How It Works

Economic Depression

What It Is and How It Works

Lisa A. Crayton and Jason Porterfield

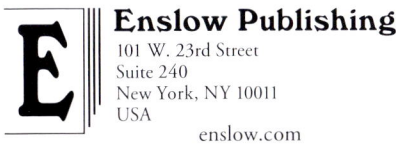

LONGWOOD PUBLIC LIBRARY

Published in 2016 by Enslow Publishing, LLC.
101 W. 23rd Street, Suite 240, New York, NY 10011

Copyright © 2016 by Enslow Publishing, LLC.

All rights reserved.

No part of this book may be reproduced by any means without the written permission of the publisher.

Library of Congress Cataloging-in-Publication Data

Crayton, Lisa A.
 Economic depression : what it is and how it works / Lisa A. Crayton and Jason Porterfield.
  pages cm. -- (Economics in the 21st century)
 Audience: Grade 9 to 12.
 Includes bibliographical references and index.
 ISBN 978-0-7660-7195-7
 1. Depressions--Juvenile literature. I. Porterfield, Jason. II. Title.
 HB3711.C685 2016
 338.5'42--dc23
                          2015028089

Printed in the United States of America

To Our Readers: We have done our best to make sure all website addresses in this book were active and appropriate when we went to press. However, the author and the publisher have no control over and assume no liability for the material available on those sites or on any sites they may link to. Any comments or suggestions can be sent by e-mail to customerservice@enslow.com.

Portions of this text were originally written by Jason Porterfield.

Photos Credits: Cover, Anastosios/Shutterstock.com (left), Tyler Olsen/Shutterstock.com (center), Everett Collection/Shutterstock.com (right); p. 6 iStock.com/Marcio Silva; p. 8 John Moore/Getty Images News/Getty Images; p. 9 Alex Wong/Getty Images News/Getty Images; p. 10 Kevin P. Casey/Bloomberg/Getty Images; p. 12 Photo12/Universal Images Group/Getty Images; p. 13 Chip Somodevilla/Getty Images News/Getty Images; p. 16 RiverNorthPhotography/iStock; p. 17 Joanne Rathe/The Boston Globe/Getty Images; p. 18 © AP Images; p. 22 Shashank Bengali/MCT/MCT/Tribune News Service/Getty Images; p. 23 Universal History Archive/Universal Image Group/Getty images; p. 28 Steve Jennings/WireImage/Getty Images; p. 30 Hulton Archive/Archive Photos/Getty Images; p. 33 General Photographic Agency/Hulton Archive/Getty Images; p. 34 FPG/Hulton Archive/Archive Photos/Getty Images; p. 38 © RosaIreneBetancourt 7/Alamy; p. 39 © Jim West/Alamy; p. 41 Scott Eells/Bloomberg/Getty Images; p. 43 Georgejmclittle/Shutterstock.com; p. 45 Universal History Archive/Universal Images Group/Getty images; p. 48 ullstein bild/Getty Images; p. 50 John Moore/Getty Images News/Getty Images; p. 51 MARK RALSTON/AFP/Getty Images; p. 53 Scott Olson/Getty Images News/Getty Images; p. 55 Patricia Marroquin/Moment Mobile/Getty Images; p. 57 Jason Andrew/Getty Images News/Getty Images; p. 59 Gabriel Hackett/Hulton Archive/Getty Images; p. 60 MPI/Archive Photos/Getty Images; p. 62 Universal History Archive/Universal Image Group/Getty Images; p. 65 The Washington Post/Getty Images; p. 67 iStock.com/Rod Kosmos; p. 72 NY Daily News/Getty Images; p. 73 iStock.com/onfilm; p. 76 Alex Wong/Getty Images News/Getty News; p. 77 Michael Nagle/Bloomberg via Getty Images.

Contents

CHAPTER 1	State of Flux	7
CHAPTER 2	Start of Depressions	26
CHAPTER 3	Depressions and Their Growth	37
CHAPTER 4	Depressions and Their Effects	49
CHAPTER 5	Recovering From a Depression	64
CHAPTER 6	Is Another Depression Likely?	70
CHAPTER 7	A Relative Calm	75
	Timeline of the History of US Depressions	80
	Bibliographic Sources	82
	Glossary	85
	Further Reading	89
	Index	93

Sometimes graphs of the highs and lows of an economy resemble the ups and downs of a roller coaster.

CHAPTER 1

State of Flux

The economy is always changing. There is no certainty when change will happen, but any movement causes the economy to either expand or contract. Graphing the up-and-down movements results in a curvy picture with high and low points that resemble the way a roller coaster moves. A roller-coaster ride is a thrilling or scary amusement park activity, depending on how you view it. Living in an ever-changing economy can prove equally thrilling or scary based on one's perspective. Economists often differ on their views of the economy, but they agree that any prolonged contraction during which the economy doesn't reboot is a depression.

A depression is *the* lowest point that the economy can drop. The United States hasn't experienced one since 1929. Many believe the nation came very close to falling into one, however, during the Great Recession. That downturn lasted from December 2007 to June 2009. Effects of the harsh economy include record levels of unemployment and home foreclosures. During the Great Recession, 8.7 million jobs were lost and more than 4 million homes fell into foreclosure, a legal process where the bank takes back a home when a homeowner cannot pay the mortgage loan. Many businesses closed and even banks failed.

In a September 2008 speech to the nation, then–President George W. Bush warned, "Our entire economy is in danger." In his speech, he made it clear

8   ECONOMIC DEPRESSION

During a depression, people struggle to find work. Entire families may become so desperate that they have to seek refuge in a homeless shelter.

that the nation's economic problems required immediate government intervention to avoid "financial panic and a distressing scenario." In late 2008, then–President-Elect Barack Obama proposed an intervention plan that worked, as discussed in Chapter Six.

Signs of Struggle

The study of the economy is usually a mix of positive and negative news. This is because even as one area of the economy is moving up, another area may be stable or heading down. Economic news abounds in the media. It is available from mobile devices, computers, televised news programs, radio programs, and other sources. During tough times, that news is usually negative. Avoiding it is not a simple matter of tuning out those sources,

During the Great Recession (December 2007–June 2009) then–President-Elect Barack Obama put forward a new intervention plan for tackling the country's economic woes.

because the reality of the economic climate affects everywhere we live, work, and play.

In the second half of 2008, every new day seemed to bring more bad economic news. People were losing their jobs, and fewer of them were able to find new work. At the same time, prices were increasing for food, gas, and other goods. Many people who borrowed money to buy a home or other large purchases in earlier years when cash and credit were flowing freely were now struggling to pay their home mortgages and other debts. Some were losing their homes. Even some banks, unable to collect on the loans they had issued, were having trouble staying open. Because of this economic turmoil, many people had to make changes in how they spent their money. These decisions affected everything from the kind of clothes

In late 2008, families that had borrowed money to buy homes were now struggling to pay their mortgages.

they bought and where they bought them to how much they drove and in what kind of car. Families skipped vacations or cut back on movies and restaurant meals.

When the economy struggles, experts try to explain why these changes occur. They see the ups and downs of the economy as part of a continuous cycle of ups and downs. These trends and cycles belong to the extraordinarily complex field of economics. Economics is the study of the way money, goods, and services are made, distributed, and bought.

National economies can go through many different stages as they react to changing conditions. For example, inflation is the general increase in the cost of goods and services for the average person. Bubbles occur when part of the economy appears healthier than it really is, while booms are the rapid growth of parts of the economy. A phenomenon called globalization refers to the interconnection of businesses and industries around the world. Recessions are usually brief economic downturns that occur when the value of a nation's goods and services declines. It often takes several months or even a couple of years for an economy to come out of a recession. Rising employment levels and greater spending by consumers usually signal the end of a recession.

If a recession lasts a very long time and keeps getting worse, it could turn into a depression. Depressions are recessions marked by very sharp, severe drops in business activity, employment, and the stock market. While economies usually come out of recessions within a year or two, depressions can last much longer.

Depressions also affect a broader range of people than a recession does. A large percentage of the population struggles with economic hardship and inflation. The most recent economic depression in the United States was the Great Depression, which lasted from 1929 to the 1940s and affected people

People struggle to find work during a depression, so historically many have headed to the employment office in search of job leads.

and nations throughout the world. While the United States eventually came out of the Great Depression, the memory of hard times lasted for decades and helped reshape the country's economic policies and institutions, many of which are still in place today.

State of Fluctuation

Different aspects of the economy, such as employment, wages, and output, are in a constant state of flux, or fluctuation—either improving or worsening, going up or going down. The economy may go through a period of incredible growth for a year or two before leveling off. The economy may stagnate, or remain relatively unchanged, and then be followed by another period of growth. It may even fall into a recession or depression. Recessions happen when the economy slows for a period of time because fewer people

In 2008, the US Senate held hearings as they tried to determine what the government could do to help a country struggling with an economic depression.

are buying goods and services, and fewer people have jobs. This results in companies producing fewer goods and offering even fewer jobs. Extremely long or severe recessions are called depressions.

Recessions often mean hard times for many people. Prices may go down but so, too, does the actual value of money. There are fewer jobs because companies aren't hiring or are even laying off their workers. The stock market declines sharply (which means the value of many companies' stocks falls). These things remain true during a depression, though to a more extreme degree.

A depression is a rare but extreme form of recession. Depressions are marked by a major and long-lasting shortfall in consumers' ability to buy goods and services, compared with the economy's potential ability to produce them. During a depression, unemployment may increase dramatically. Lenders stop offering people credit (the ability to obtain cash or buy things on the promise of repayment in the future). Fewer people invest their money in the stock market, and the value of money itself goes down. Prices fall as demand for goods evaporates. People's assets, such as their homes, lose value. Less buying and selling takes place and bankruptcies rise.

The economy becomes stuck in this cycle because vast numbers of people—many of them unemployed, working for less than they used to, or worried about losing their jobs—can't afford goods and services. At the same time, companies aren't hiring people because they aren't making any money when their products are going unsold. It often takes years and dramatic change sparked by the government or outside events for an economy to climb out of a depression. Government intervention in a depressed economy can include large public spending and building projects, cash "bailouts" of struggling industries, the setting of lower interest rates to make loans cheaper, and taxpayer relief in the form of tax cuts or rebates.

Indicating the Economy

The words *depression* and *recession* both describe economic downturns. Generally, recessions that are very severe or last for a very long time are considered depressions. It isn't always clear how they are different. For example, until the Great Depression of the 1930s, any downturn in the United States economy was called a depression. At that time, economists came up with the word *recession* to describe less severe downturns than the one the United States was experiencing.

Today, experts use statistics and data called economic indicators to judge the economy's performance. Economic indicators reflect how well certain parts of the economy are performing. The unemployment rate is one such number. The unemployment rate measures the number of people who do not have jobs but are looking for work. A low unemployment rate shows that companies are doing well and hiring workers.

A rising unemployment rate often means that some companies are shedding workers while others are simply not hiring. This can be a strong sign that the economy is weakening.

Inflation refers to the rising cost of goods and services over a period of time. It can also mean the decreasing value of money. In both cases, goods and services become more expensive, either because their sticker prices are rising or because your dollar is worth less than it used to be. It buys less than it did before the inflationary period began. During a period of inflation, it takes more money to buy things than it did before. Economists generally agree that inflation happens when the money supply grows faster than the economy grows. There is too much money in circulation in the economy (perhaps because of easy loans and credit and rising wages) and not enough production of goods and services. So, demand is high, supply is low, and

The prices of goods, such as gasoline, and services may rise over time during inflation. Soon consumers' dollars don't buy as much gas as they did during better economic times.

prices rise. When there is a lot of money in circulation, its value—its actual purchasing power—decreases.

Two of the most important economic indicators are numbers called the gross national product and the gross domestic product. The gross national product (GNP) is the market value of all final goods and services made using resources owned by people of that economy. These resources can include materials, stores, or factories that are located in other countries. So, an American-based company that sells clothing in France made from Chinese silk and manufactured in Indian factories contributes to the GNP of the United States. The GNP of the United States can include cars or other factory goods produced by American companies in other parts of the world.

Don't Bury Your Head

To explain why they don't keep up with economic news and issues, some people say they prefer to hide like an ostrich by burying their head in the sand. But guess what? It is a myth that ostriches behave like that when fearful!

It's important to talk about any questions and worries you might have about the economy.

Don't be afraid to know what's really happening around you. Use these methods to boost your knowledge and courage.

1. **Talk about it.** Share your questions, concerns, and thoughts with a parent or teacher.

2. **Know the facts.** Rely only on reputable news sources.

3. **Help arrange a school visit.** Talk to your teacher about bringing an economist into your classroom.

4. **Visit.** Arrange a meeting to visit an economist's job.

5. **Check your network.** Ask family members, teachers, neighbors, and friends if they know professionals willing to provide resources, chat with you, or visit your school.

ECONOMIC DEPRESSION

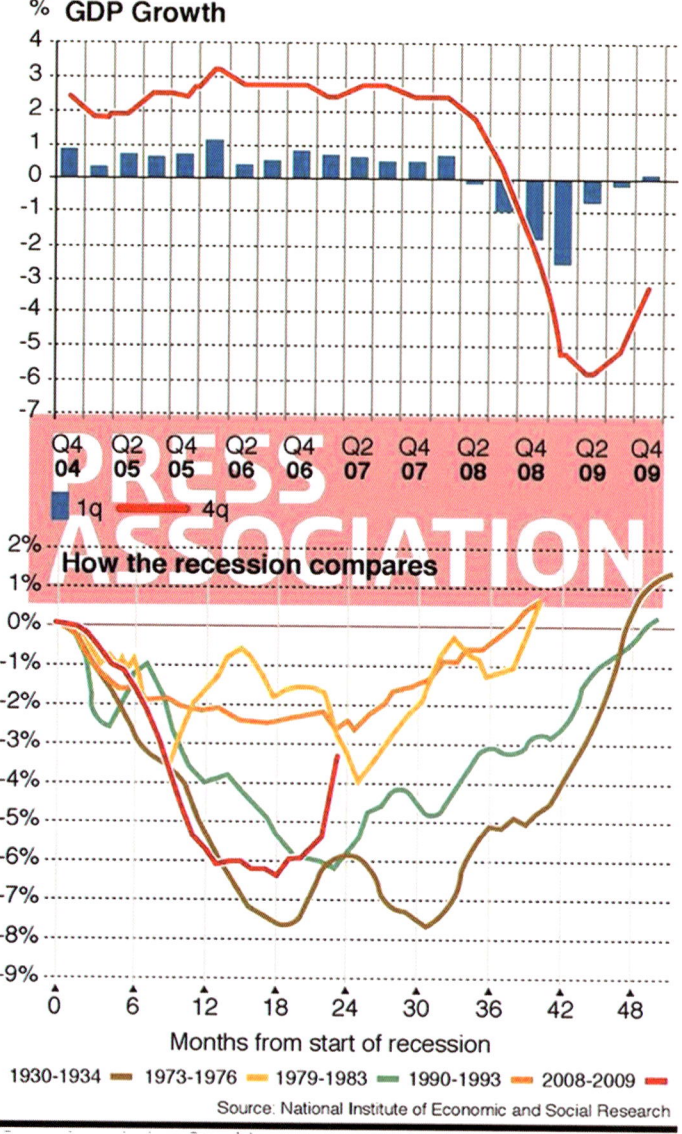

This graph shows gross domestic product (GDP) figures from the Office of National Statistics. It compares the 2009 recession with past recessions in the United Kingdom.

The gross domestic product (GDP) represents a part of the GNP. It stands for the total value of all final goods and services at current market prices produced within an economy within a given year. In this case, the goods and services must be produced on American soil.

Both the GDP and the GNP are important numbers for economists because they reflect the health of the economy. If these numbers go up over a period of time, it means that the economy is generally strong. If their rate of increase slows, it shows that the growth of the economy itself is slowing, and there may be trouble on the way. A drop in these numbers could signal the beginning of a recession. If the GDP drops by more than 10 percent, it signals the beginning of a depression.

Explaining the Business Cycle

Economists explain the ups and downs of the economy as simply being a part of the business cycle. Business cycles are made up of four phases: peak, recession, trough, and recovery. Economists cannot predict the exact phases of a cycle or say how long they may last. However, the economy is always in one of these four phases. Recall that when shown on a graph, these phases look like a roller coaster. The cycle begins with a peak. It drops with a recession. When it hits the trough, it starts climbing again as it recovers. It reaches another peak, and the cycle starts again.

Peaks occur when the economy is performing near its highest possible level. Economists use economic indicators to figure out whether the economy is trending upward or downward. Economists consider the economy strong if unemployment is low and the GDP is rising. In a peak, the GDP has reached its maximum.

The peak ends when the economy starts to contract, or shrink. The economy enters a recession at this point. A recession is a downturn in the business cycle. The GDP declines during a recession. Corporate profits may also go down. At the same time, unemployment may go up, as fewer people looking for work are able to find jobs. In the most extreme cases, recessions become depressions.

Ultimately, the economy will reach a point where unemployment stops increasing and economic output stops decreasing. This point is the trough, the third stage of the business cycle. The trough is the bottom of the business cycle. The length of time between the peak and the trough marks how long the recession has lasted. The trough represents both good and bad news for the economy. On one hand, it is the lowest point in the business cycle and represents its worst conditions. On the other hand, it also marks the beginning of the last phase of the business cycle, the recovery period.

During the recovery period, the economy once again begins growing, sometimes vigorously. Companies start hiring again, and people begin spending more money. Production is increased to meet this rising demand, resulting in more hiring and more consumer spending. A positive cycle begins and gathers momentum. The economy may even enter a boom period, in which it grows very rapidly. The economy begins working its way to another peak, at which point the business cycle starts over and again begins its inevitable move downward.

Past Depressions

The last major economic depression to hit the United States began in the late-1920s and ended around the beginning of the 1940s. The economy has not come close to such a major economic collapse since. However, during the nineteenth century, recessions and even depressions were quite common.

Often, depressions would be set off by a panic of some kind. Banks might suddenly discover that they had overextended credit and could not collect the money owed them. As a result, they'd be forced to close. Or, stock traders might manipulate the market by offering useless stocks or properties at high prices. Once the real value of these items became apparent, prices would collapse and people would lose fortunes. A ripple effect of plummeting stock prices and investor panic would spread throughout the economy, damaging even previously healthy companies. During this period, the government did very little to regulate the economy, and bank and stock market mismanagement and panics were relatively common.

During the nineteenth century, five major financial panics hit the United States: in 1819, 1837, 1857, 1873, and 1893. All five led to depressions. The Panic of 1819 resulted in the first depression in US history. The economy had been struggling since the United States went to war with Great Britain in the War of 1812 (1812–1814). At the time, cotton was one of the country's biggest exports and a key part of the economy. Cotton prices fell sharply in 1819. At the same time, credit froze, and banks and lenders were forced to call in loans. Farms were foreclosed (taken over by the banks that farmers owed money to), and many banks collapsed during the panic. The panic lasted until 1821.

Several factors caused the Panic of 1837. Cotton prices had again collapsed. Wheat crops had failed. Land speculation (in which people rapidly purchased and sold overvalued land in the hope of making a profit) resulted in a burst real estate bubble and the loss of investments. The variety of

The Panic of 1837 was in part caused by a severe drop in the prices of cotton.

currency circulating in the United States (at the time, many states issued their own currency) caused confusion and inflation. Financial problems in Great Britain had ripple effects in the United States. The depression that resulted from all of these stresses was the second longest in the country's history, lasting for about six years. Many financial firms in New York City and state-sponsored banks failed, and the cost of labor dropped sharply. Real estate and food prices also dropped. Land speculators who had bought acreage at high prices were wiped out, as were farmers and planters who couldn't get decent prices for their crops.

The Panic of 1857, in contrast, was triggered by a single event—the collapse of the Ohio Life Insurance and Trust Company. The company, which mostly operated out of New York City, had over-speculated on railroads before collapsing. Stock prices of other companies plummeted when the company collapsed. More than nine hundred investment firms failed because of the panic. The economy didn't begin recovering until 1859.

Railroad speculation also set off the Panic of 1873. The investment firm Jay Cooke and Company collapsed, causing the stock market to drop and many businesses to fail. About three million American workers lost their jobs because of the panic. Food prices fell sharply. Many farmers once again couldn't get good prices for their crops, causing widespread poverty in farming communities. The depression lasted for five years, ending in 1878.

THE GREAT RACE FOR THE WESTERN STAKES 1870

Railroad speculation was another spark that helped fire up the Panic of 1873. This illustration shows Cornelius Vanderbilt and James Fisk competing for control of the railroads of New York.

The Panic of 1893 was the last depression to hit the country during the nineteenth century. It was also the worst in the country's history until the Great Depression. The stock market dropped that spring and then crashed in June, as panicked stockholders sold off their shares. By the end of the year, more than sixteen thousand businesses had failed. Among the failed businesses were 153 railroads and nearly 500 banks. Unemployment climbed until one in six Americans was unemployed. The depression finally ended in 1897.

Ten Great Questions to Ask a Financial Adviser

1. How do depressions begin?
2. How long can a depression last?
3. How can I protect my savings and investments during a depression?
4. How do I know that a depression has ended?
5. Why don't more recessions turn into depressions?
6. What laws and regulations protect the economy from a depression?
7. Who decides that a depression has begun or ended?
8. Will another depression happen in the United States?
9. How is the US economy linked to the economies of other countries?
10. How do financial recoveries begin?

CHAPTER 2

Start of Depressions

ealth professionals ask lots of questions during routine and emergency visits. Those center about the "5W's and H"—who, what, when, where, why, and how pain, illness, or physical discomfort happened. They may ask: Who was involved? (Perhaps you caught the flu from your sibling or parent.) What is wrong? When did the pain or condition start? Where does it hurt? Why did it happen? (Did you have an accident at school, home, or work?) How do you feel? (Pain is often measured on a scale of one to ten in rising intensity). The goal is to determine the *root* of the problem to properly assess and treat it. In the same way, economists search for the root of an economic depression to make accurate predictions.

It often seems as if economic depressions are set off by a single event. The stock market fails, and many investors lose money. A major industry may collapse and suddenly put thousands of people out of work. The beginning of a depression may be marked by bank failures or a sudden tightening of credit. While these dramatic events may appear to be the cause, they often follow other economic troubles that may have been brewing for months or even years before the depression hits.

How Depressions Start

Prices for goods and services rise and fall over time. Economists call these changes "fluctuations." Local fluctuations are price changes for goods that are sold in their country of origin. International price fluctuations happen to goods that are exported and sold in other countries.

Often, price fluctuations follow the law of supply and demand. They may rise when there is a shortage or if a product is new. Prices fall when the market is flooded with a product or service, as companies compete for customers who have a wide range of choices. Many companies export goods to sell in other countries. These companies can make large profits if there's not already a similar product for sale on the local market and the demand is high. However, if the demand weakens, it may no longer be worthwhile to spend the money to ship a product overseas.

Both local and international price fluctuations can impact the nation's economy. Local fluctuations affect the ability of people to buy goods and services. They also affect the ability of business owners to make a profit. During recessions and depressions, people often cut back on buying things they don't really need. Businesses often lower prices to attract increasingly scarce buyers. Charging less may attract some customers, but it also reduces profits.

Price fluctuations also affect the job market. If fewer people are buying a company's products, prices fall and profits decrease, and the company may cut its workforce. Many companies severely cut production during the Great Depression. Unemployment rose because of these production cuts. By cutting production, companies saved money they would have otherwise spent on raw materials and labor. Yet, they also limited the number of their products available for sale to consumers. This further damaged their chances of profiting from their products. Another factor that can help cause a depression is inflation.

Smart Shopping

High prices during an economic depression force consumers to make tough decisions about their needs and wants. They weigh whether buying a cup of coffee they want for more than four dollars is prudent given the skyrocketing cost of food, gas, clothing, and other needed items. All of that changes when the economy improves. People spend more on nonessentials, feeling at ease about their financial situations.

During an economic depression, consumers check around for the best deals. Some apps help find bargains and sales.

In any economic condition, however, getting a good deal is important. Today, people use smartphone apps to track price fluctuations, comparing the cost of identical items at competing retailers—or even different locations of the same retailer. This smart shopping technique pays off in additional savings when the person heads to the store with the cheapest price—or not. As the popularity of the bargain hunting tool picked up, so has the number of retailers willing to match lower prices when shown app price differences.

Inflation happens in two ways. Prices for most products can go up beyond what people are used to spending for them, or their money could drop in value (it is worth less and can buy less than before). Sometimes, both things occur together. In either case, people can no longer buy products for the same relatively low price they might have paid before. Stores and businesses may have to close because people can no longer afford their increasingly expensive products or services.

Natural disasters and wars also play a role in the beginnings of depressions. Many of the depressions of the nineteenth century were caused by droughts or crop failures. Wars can help bring on depressions when fighting destroys factories, farmland, and materials. Countries at war may have to borrow money from other countries to pay for the expenses of continued fighting. Repaying the debt can severely stress a nation already battered by war. Yet, ironically, wars can also help end depressions by putting people to work making things like weapons, armored vehicles, aircraft, ships, and uniforms.

Events taking place in other parts of the world can also help cause recessions and depressions. During the 1920s, much of Europe was still recovering from World War I. Factories in many European countries had been damaged by the war, and these countries had to import goods from the United States to rebuild. The United States profited greatly from this trade imbalance at first. But when European economies collapsed, American companies lost much of their export business.

The Great Depression's Genesis

The 1920s were a booming time for the United States. While much of Europe was struggling to recover from World War I, the United States was experiencing tremendous economic growth. Jobs were plentiful, and

During the "Roaring '20s" the US economy was growing. Many jobs were available and prices were good. People had money to spend.

high production made goods affordable to many people. Money became a sign of success, and business leaders were widely admired. Stocks soared in value as more Americans invested, hoping to get rich. Many people, even wealthy and savvy businessmen, made risky stock investments in hopes of making a large profit.

On October 24, 1929, the stock market crashed, and millions of people lost money. The day went down in history as "Black Thursday." For many people, this represents the beginning of the Great Depression. Yet, Black Thursday was not the end of the slide. Stocks kept dropping in value for the rest of the month as panicked investors tried to sell off their increasingly devalued shares.

At first, the market crash didn't directly affect many families. Most average Americans didn't own stocks. Many who did held on to them, hoping that the market would recover. Retail sales remained strong through the end of the year as people kept buying products. Many people thought that the downturn would end soon.

Though most Americans had not been affected yet, many felt uneasy after the crash. They wondered what had caused it, and many different theories and explanations were put forward. President Herbert Hoover, who had been elected in 1928, blamed the lingering aftereffects of World War I. He also criticized stock market speculators who had hoped to make quick profits selling their stock at high prices. Others blamed the government for allowing businesses to merge into monopolies. They also blamed the government for allowing banks and other lenders to expand and contract credit for profit. Still others felt that too much of the country's wealth was concentrated in the hands of just a few rich people.

The Depression Lingers

At first, it appeared the depression might end quickly. President Hoover acted to kick-start the economy by lowering taxes and asking businesses to keep wages at pre-crash levels. Many businesses did so, and some even raised wages for their workers.

Keeping wages high didn't hold off a growing economic slowdown, however. Many businesses were forced to cut workers as they cut production. Because more people lost their jobs, fewer people had money to buy products. People who still had jobs stopped buying things, even though prices had started falling. They were afraid that they, too, would soon lose their jobs and wanted to save as much as possible in case of emergency. This was a complete reversal from spending patterns in the 1920s, when many Americans enthusiastically bought things on credit while the economy was good and jobs were secure.

Bank failures shook the country's confidence. Many banks began calling in loans. People didn't have the money to repay what they owed. When people who had money in savings accounts heard that their bank might be struggling, many panicked and took their money out all at once. If enough bank customers did this, there was a "run on the bank." Lines formed outside of banks, as panicked depositors tried to withdraw all of their savings. Banks often failed or closed and locked their doors until the panic subsided. Many banks failed, with 659 banks closing in 1929 alone.

People who had money in banks that failed saw their savings wiped out. This was a huge additional blow to people who had already lost their jobs or suddenly needed to repay loans. Banks became less willing to risk their

President Herbert Hoover tried to give the ailing economy a much-needed boost with acts such as lowering taxes.

When people were worried that their bank might be struggling, almost everyone tried to clean out his or her bank account, which was called a "run on the bank."

financial well-being by loaning money to people. Companies that relied on short-term loans to pay workers could no longer do so. They also had no access to loans that would allow them to maintain equipment and facilities, expand operations, or develop new products. Individual borrowers could no longer obtain cash to buy houses or other goods and services. Money stopped circulating in the economy and spending dried up, which forced companies to cut production and jobs even further.

Investments also slowed, draining even more money out of the economy and stifling business development. This was the case, even though the stock market had rebounded to early 1929 levels by the spring of 1930. Gross investment in the United States had fallen by 35 percent between 1929 and 1930. Investment had almost slowed to a trickle by 1931. That year, $800 million was invested, down from $16.2 billion in 1929.

These drops in spending and investing made an already bad situation even worse. Business leaders saw their unsold products sitting on shelves and cut production further. As more people lost their jobs, demand for products fell even more. Many businesses took steps to prepare for the worst. They continued to cut production and prices and stopped buying materials from other businesses. These were logical steps for them to take to survive. Yet, when thousands of businesses took these steps at the same time, it gravely weakened the economy.

Myths and Facts

Myth: A depression is a normal part of the business cycle.

Fact: While recessions are part of the normal business cycle, depressions are extremely severe economic downturns that take years for the economy to overcome and recover from.

Myth: The stock market crash of 1929 caused the Great Depression.

Fact: While the stock market set off a panic, the economy was already struggling when the market crashed.

Myth: A depression in one country won't affect the rest of the world.

Fact: Global economies are closely linked through international trade, and serious problems in one country can often set off trouble around the world.

CHAPTER 3

Depressions and Their Growth

Despite the bumpy, roller-coaster feel to the economy as the business cycle runs its course, recessions are simply part of the cycle. They are usually short lived. Countries rebound from them in a matter of months. Positive signs are increases in productivity, hiring, and consumer spending. Wage increases and readily available credit are two reasons consumers spend more. They are more hopeful and relaxed about economic conditions. This consumer confidence impacts supply and demand, and the economy responds by moving upward. Coming out a depressions isn't as easy because the downturn is steeper and more prolonged. It was tough for the United States to climb out of the Great Depression because of its severity and length.

During a depression, economic indicators show that the economy is contracting. This means that the economy is continuing to get worse. Manufacturers produce less, businesses earn less, people spend less, and more workers become and remain unemployed. While these factors are also true of a recession, they either continue for a much longer period of time or are much worse during a depression.

As a depression lingers, families and children feel its effects.

A Deeper Depression

Even as the depression deepened in 1930, the situation didn't seem any worse to some Americans than it had been during the last recession. Just before the economic boom of the 1920s began, the country had suffered through a recession that lasted from 1920 to 1921. Unemployment had averaged 11.9 percent during that time. By the end of 1930, the unemployment rate had not reached 9 percent yet. The Great Depression would not fully set in until 1931, when it became a global problem.

In the fall of 1930, President Hoover formed a committee called the President's Committee for Employment in an attempt to end the crisis. The organization did very little to help the situation. It failed to gather any real statistics on the economic crisis or organize any relief efforts. Instead, it focused mostly on trying to restore the public's confidence in the economy.

DEPRESSIONS AND THEIR GROWTH 39

When the federal government can't offer relief, local and state governments must cope, often by cutting services. People protest cuts to public facilities and social services.

President Hoover and his government opposed federal relief efforts. They thought that people without jobs could still somehow get by without relief and government assistance.

With the federal government checked out, local and state governments were left to pick up the slack and deal with the needs of the growing number of unemployed people. By 1932, these governments had run out of funds. Raising state taxes was not an option, since many citizens would be unwilling and unable to pay. Some states issued bonds for sale in an effort to raise money, but few people were willing to buy them. (Bonds are certificates that governments sell to citizens to help fund public projects. Someone who buys a bond is promised a profit on his or her investment after a certain period of time has passed.) Many states also had laws forbidding their governments to operate with unbalanced budgets (meaning that they couldn't spend more than they took in). In 1932, only eight states offered any sort of relief payments to unemployed workers.

A Rigid Standard

When the Great Depression first began in 1929, the value of the US dollar was directly linked to the value of gold. This "gold standard" meant that people could take their paper money or bonds into a bank and have it redeemed for an equivalent amount of actual gold. Many of the world's economies at the time were based on the gold standard. The value of gold linked these economies together.

One problem with the gold standard was that it made the money supply very rigid. If governments printed money beyond the value of the gold held in banks, the money would lose value because it couldn't all be redeemed for gold. If people started to hoard money during these times when it became

Because the economy was based on the gold standard in 1929, the government couldn't print money beyond the gold they had, or the paper money would lose value.

less valuable, waiting for its value to increase again, there would be a physical shortage of cash available. The gold standard also linked world economies closely together based on the global value of gold. Cash shortages in one country could affect the value of gold worldwide. Likewise, the number of people trading in their cash for gold would also affect its value.

After a wave of bank failures in some parts of Europe, problems soon spread to Great Britain, as worried people pulled their money out of British banks. The British pound was one of the most important currencies in the world and was linked to the value of many other currencies around the world. But people afraid of a bank collapse sought the safety of actual, physical wealth (rather than paper currency) and withdrew their gold from banks in large numbers. As a result, the pound lost value, and Great Britain was forced to stop using the gold standard in September 1931. From then on, British bank customers were not able to exchange paper currency for the equivalent amount of gold.

When Great Britain went off the gold standard, many other countries were also forced to abandon it. In the United States, however, the country's Federal Reserve (a federal agency that acts as the country's central bank) moved to keep the gold standard. The Federal Reserve had to cut the money supply—the amount of money in circulation. This was necessary because the amount of money in circulation (currency) had to equal the amount of US gold reserves in banks. At this time, there was more currency in circulation than there was gold to back it. Siphoning this excess currency out of circulation meant raising interest rates on loans. This made it more expensive for people to borrow money, so soon less money was in circulation. This led to deflation—scarcity of cash, decreased purchasing, a wholesale drop in prices, and a drop in production.

Banks called in loans, and customers postponed buying things until they had more cash and in the hope of even lower prices ahead. Yet, the fall in production led to layoffs and higher unemployment and even less spending. In many cases, banks had to foreclose on homes because people couldn't pay their debts. Within the next two years, more than half a million mortgages would be foreclosed (which meant that people lost their homes). As news and rumors spread about banks struggling because of loans not being repaid, depositors began to withdraw their money, fearing that their savings would be lost if the bank failed. This led to even more bank collapses. More than five hundred US banks failed in just the first month after Britain went off the gold standard. By the end of 1931, there had been 2,293 bank failures in the United States.

Just Click and Apply

Some people prefer to pay for everything in cash. Many save months or years to do so. Others take a different route. When people need extra cash to purchase a home, buy a car, pay for tuition, pay for a family vacation, or reduce high-interest credit cards, they apply for loans. Technology has changed a complex, time-consuming process to one that happens in mere minutes when done over the Internet. Rather than visiting a bank or credit union, a consumer can visit the website of a preferred financial institution and fill out a loan application. Shortly after clicking and applying, the potential borrower receives the answer. If the answer is positive and depending on the institution, the monies for the purchase may be available in hours. That's an amazing turn-around time given the time it took to process a loan decades ago.

Today's technology makes it possible to apply for a much-needed loan by just filling out a quick form online.

The Dust Bowl

A severe drought struck parts of the Midwestern and Great Plains states in 1930 and lasted until 1936 in many parts of the region. Farmers who had already been struggling with low crop prices saw their crops wither and their soil turn to dust and blow away. Much of the region's topsoil had been weakened by poor farming practices over several decades. High prairie winds would come and blow the topsoil away. At times, the clouds of dust blackened the sky.

Millions of acres of farmland were rendered useless by the drought. Hundreds of thousands of people, sometimes called Okies because many came from hard-hit Oklahoma, were forced to leave their homes. Many ended up working for very low pay picking fruit and other crops on the West Coast. They often faced discrimination and rough treatment. Author John Steinbeck documented the plight of the Okies in his classic novel *The Grapes of Wrath*, while folk singer Woody Guthrie sang songs about the Dust Bowl on his album *Dust Bowl Ballads*.

In 1935, clouds of dust engulfed the Plains states, blackening the sky, ruining farmland, and causing some people to flee their homes.

Meanwhile, unemployment continued to rise. By the end of 1931, unemployment in the United States had risen to 15.9 percent. The country faced economic problems far worse than anything it had ever faced before. Tax receipts for the federal government fell by $900 million, while expenses rose by $200 million. The federal budget went into a deficit of millions of dollars. A deficit means that the government is spending more money than it is receiving in a given period of time, such as a year.

Today, it is common for the government to continue spending money, even when there is a budget deficit. But at the time of the Great Depression, balancing the budget seemed like an important first step in fixing the economy. In late 1931, Hoover asked Congress to pass a tax increase to balance the budget. The higher taxes placed an even greater burden on people who were out of work or still employed but struggling with lower wages and devalued currency.

The Trouble With Tariffs

In the postwar years—after World War I but before the Great Depression—the United States had profited greatly from selling goods to a war-ravaged Europe. At the same time, the US government had imposed high tariffs on foreign goods. Tariffs are taxes on imports from other countries. They are meant to protect domestic businesses by making goods from overseas more expensive for people to buy.

In 1927, a world economic conference had ended with many governments agreeing to stop imposing tariffs on foreign goods. The idea was that world trade would improve if there were fewer tariffs and, as a result, the world economy would experience healthy growth.

Many business and government leaders in the United States, however, still supported tariffs. They felt that tariffs protected domestic companies by making their products more competitive. After the stock market crash of 1929, business leaders in the United States pushed the government to set another tariff, despite the 1927 agreement. The result was a tariff bill called the Smoot-Hawley Tariff, passed in 1930. According to the US Department of State website, Hoover had originally meant for the tariff to help protect farmers, but it had the opposite affect:

> The Smoot-Hawley Tariff Act of June 1930 raised U.S. tariffs to historically high levels. The original intention behind the legislation was to increase the protection afforded domestic farmers against foreign agricultural imports. . . . But once the tariff schedule revision process got started, it proved impossible to stop. Calls for increased protection flooded in from industrial sector special interest groups, and soon a bill meant to provide relief for farmers became a means to raise tariffs in all sectors of the economy.

Other nations resented the new tariff. Many of these countries owed money to the United States and couldn't hope to pay their debts unless they could sell their products to American consumers. The United States was the biggest foreign market at that time. In retaliation, European countries passed their own tariff laws against the United States. As a consequence of the new global tariffs, world trade fell sharply. This made it harder for manufacturers, farmers, and others to sell their goods overseas and made the depression worse for people all around the world.

Franklin Delano Roosevelt's New Deal program offered relief, but it would be another ten years before the economy completely recovered.

By 1933, the consumer price index (a statistic that measures average prices for goods) in the United States had dropped 18 percent from 1929 levels. Falling prices made it hard for businesses to keep their wages at the same level, as they had promised in 1929. Many of the country's largest corporations, such as US Steel and Ford, started cutting wages in 1931. By the time Franklin Delano Roosevelt (known as FDR) took office as president in 1933, the country's GDP had fallen from $103.6 billion to $56.4 billion. Even with the extensive relief efforts that were part of FDR's New Deal program, it took the economy ten years to make up this lost ground in American productivity.

CHAPTER 4
Depressions and Their Effects

Depressions are particularly troublesome because they linger for a long time. Their effects propel people to discover inventive ways of surviving financial hardship. Spending habits change, reflecting a switch to thrifty money management. People still talk about some ways family members survived during the Great Depression. The stories reflect the fear, anguish, and despair felt during that grueling time in our nation's history.

People who live through them often have vivid memories of trying to survive the long, lean years. They may remember family members losing their jobs or ending up jobless themselves. People who were children at the time may remember their parents worrying about buying food or paying the bills. Many survivors of severe economic depressions alter their spending patterns for decades after recovery, remaining extremely careful with their money for the rest of their lives.

In the short term, people often have to make serious sacrifices during a depression. Families cut their spending on all but the most necessary goods. Today, modern families would likely cut back on things like Internet connections, cable television, vacations, and clothes and toy shopping. They may drive less or get rid of their second car to save money on gas,

People who survive depressions often change spending and saving habits. Always mindful of how they or their parents struggled just to keep food on the table, they share their stories.

repairs, and insurance. Families may also sell off their prized possessions like vacation homes, boats, jewelry, or family heirlooms to make ends meet. If a parent's wages or hours are cut or if a family member loses his or her job, younger members of the family may have to look for work to help the family get by.

Unemployment's Impact

Rising unemployment both contributes to a depression and indicates that an economic slump is taking place. A rising unemployment rate reveals that businesses are not hiring new workers as well as cutting their workforce.

The effects of rising unemployment can be far-reaching. A higher unemployment rate means that more workers are jobless and looking for employment. Without their paychecks, they have very little to spend. Even

DEPRESSIONS AND THEIR EFFECTS
51

People want to work, but during a depression jobs are scarce. When they lose their jobs, they lose their paychecks and struggle to make ends meet.

workers who still have their jobs contribute to the continued slump. They may save more of their money rather than spending it, fearful that they, too, will soon lose their jobs. During depressions, unemployment may reach into the double digits. During the Great Depression, unemployment peaked at around 25 percent in 1933, which means that one out of every four American workers was out of a job.

Diminishing Demand

Demand for products falls during depressions. People spend their money only on things that they really need and cut back on or eliminate unessential purchases. They may put off buying new clothes and instead repair their clothes or change their eating habits by buying less expensive food. Big-ticket and luxury items are among the first to be cut out of budgets. Families put off buying new cars or appliances, such as refrigerators.

With demand for their products falling, manufacturers are forced to cut production and jobs. This affects other industries as well. When business slows and cash gets tight, companies cut back on the purchasing of goods and services from other businesses—for example, office equipment and supplies, manufacturing equipment, and accountants.

Widespread Bankruptcies

In a depression, creditors—institutions or individuals who loan money—often call in their debts in an effort to keep money moving in and out of the firm smoothly. They may also call in their loans if they hear that a business is in trouble and may be unable to pay. With business down, the debtor cannot afford to pay off all of his or her loans and may be forced to declare bankruptcy.

Bankruptcy is a legally declared inability of a person or organization to pay off creditors. Declaring bankruptcy is a way to assure creditors that their loans will be paid off. It gives the lender and debtor an opportunity to come up with a payment plan and realistic repayment schedule that will satisfy the lenders and give the debtors some extra time and breathing room. In a worst-case scenario, the person or business owner may have to sell off assets like real estate, office equipment, or even the business itself to pay off his or her debts.

Not only businesses can declare bankruptcy. Individuals can, too, when they fall too far behind in their debts. Bankruptcy does not wipe away debt or free you from repaying it. It simply gives you more time to do so and may reduce the amount owed somewhat. The drawback is that you will be considered much less creditworthy in the future and will probably have trouble obtaining loans, mortgages, and credit cards.

Businesses also suffer during a depression. When they can't pay their bills they may be forced to declare bankruptcy just to cope with mounting debt.

Credit Crunch

Credit problems are another factor that can both signal the beginning of an economic slump and contribute further to the downturn. Before the Great Depression began, people had freely borrowed money to purchase homes and new and expensive technological wonders, such as automobiles, refrigerators, and radios. At the time, banks and other creditors had the fluidity to make these loans because cash was flowing freely throughout the expanding economy. But when the stock market collapsed and creditors started calling in loans, many people couldn't pay them back. Banks collapsed, and bankers became much less willing to risk lending money again for much of the rest of the depression years.

The restricted credit harmed the economy in several ways. People could no longer borrow money to purchase goods, nor could they borrow money to help pay off their other debts. Businesses also had a much harder time borrowing money. Businesses often rely on short-term loans to pay workers and buy supplies and materials. They use their product stock as a guarantee that they can pay the loan. For example, a store may use the value of its merchandise as a guarantee or proof that it can repay the loan it is asking for. But if businesses can't borrow money, they can't pay workers or purchase materials for the manufacture of their products, and business grinds to a halt. This tends to deepen the slump.

Fluctuating Prices

Prices for goods generally tend to drop during depressions. This sounds like good news, as it would make it easier for people with little money to make purchases. However, it actually spells trouble for the economy. Sellers

The E-Commerce Effect

Decreased consumer demand places stores at greater risk of closing. Ironically, increased demand for online shopping is having the same effect on retail chains around the country. This trend is called e-commerce. It attracts people who want to shop at favorite venues. It affects stores of all sizes, including mom-and-pop shops, large retail chains, and specialty boutiques because today people can buy virtually anything online. Stores often match prices in both settings or use special discounts to draw consumers to shop either online or in-store. At one time, many store owners thought e-commerce would sharply increase profits. That is not the case. E-commerce has, instead, rocked in-store sales, plummeting profits and contributing to store closures.

When consumers are spending less, demand decreases and business may be forced to close their doors.

are forced to lower prices on their goods to attract buyers. They may have to drop prices to the point where they are forced to sell their products at a loss. If they keep losing money this way, businesses may eventually be forced to close.

Lower prices do not just apply to goods and services. They can also mean lower wages and lower values for homes. If workers receive lower wages, they do not have as much money to spend on goods and services. This can also hurt businesses further. Unfortunately, a price that does not drop is the amount of debt that a person owes on loans to banks or credit card companies. There's also the chance that some goods could actually go up in price, even during a depression. Shortages sometimes happen during depressions. Business owners who make or sell a product that's in high demand may take advantage of the situation by raising prices, especially if that product is considered essential, such as bread, eggs, meat, or fuel.

Social Discord

Depressions are often marked by social unrest, and sometimes major changes take place in society as a result. During these times, people feel frightened and insecure. They may be angry at the government for mishandling the economy or resent the wealthy who don't share their hardships. People hungry for change may switch political parties and take their anger out on politicians by voting them out of office.

During the Great Depression, angry voters blamed President Herbert Hoover, a member of the Republican Party, for the country's economic

DEPRESSIONS AND THEIR EFFECTS   57

When people aren't happy with the government or the president, they might express their displeasure with public demonstrations.

problems. They also blamed Republican members of Congress. Republicans had controlled both the presidency and Congress all through the 1920s. Republicans lost control of both the House and the Senate in the midterm election of 1930. In 1932, Hoover himself lost the presidential election in a landslide to Democrat Franklin Delano Roosevelt.

Other public demonstrations of dissatisfaction are not as peaceful, orderly, and civic-minded as voting. In past depressions, riots have been common responses to foreclosures and shortages. Sometimes, mobs stormed and occupied public buildings to protest government policies. The unemployed may march in demonstrations. In the past, demonstrators have clashed with police and even the military during depressions, sometimes resulting in death and injury.

Crime may also rise during depressions. Desperate people may go outside of the law to make money or obtain food, robbing banks, committing burglaries, or shoplifting. Violent crimes like murders may also increase. During the Great Depression, for example, bank robbers like John Dillinger and the famous duo of Bonnie Parker and Clyde Barrow captured the public's imagination by robbing the banks that some people blamed for causing the depression and seizing their homes, farms, or savings. These violent criminals were almost beloved figures, mistakenly regarded by many struggling and angry Americans as modern-day Robin Hoods, stealing from the rich and giving to the poor.

How People Fared

Life for many Americans changed drastically during the Great Depression. Many were out of work and struggled to buy food and other necessities. Many people had a hard time finding enough to eat. One study conducted

The Bonus Army

One of the largest demonstrations to take place during the Great Depression was a June 1932 march on Washington, DC, by about twenty thousand World War I veterans. They marched to ask the government to pay them bonuses that had been promised to them for their service. The bonuses were not supposed to come due until 1945, but many of the veterans needed the money immediately to survive the depression. The Senate refused to allow the early payments.

Many of the veterans left, but about four thousand stayed behind and rioted on July 28. Soldiers were called in to drive them out and destroy their camp using tanks and tear gas. The group finally left after Congress appropriated $100,000 to send them home. Congress eventually voted to allow cash payments of the bonuses in 1936.

In June, 1932, twenty thousand veterans, frantic for a bonus promised by the government, marched in protest. The Senate refused to pay early, and on July 28 many desperate veterans rioted.

During the Great Depression, people who lost their livelihoods and their homes moved to settlements called "Hoovervilles," which popped up on city edges. Without help from the Hoover administration, people were impoverished.

at the time found that families with at least one fully employed member had 66 percent less illness than families in which no one was working. Some people living in rural areas sometimes ate weeds to survive. People living in cities sometimes had to dig through garbage cans and city dumps for food.

As unemployment grew, many men started traveling in search of work, sometimes hopping trains to cover greater distances. By 1932, men dressed in battered clothing and seeking work were common sights in many cities and towns. Often, these wandering men were discriminated against by people who thought they were trying to take jobs from working people in the town. At worst, they were seen as potentially dangerous drifters or even classified by local laws as vagrants and subject to arrest and imprisonment. Settlements of unemployed men and impoverished, homeless families living in crude shacks—called "Hoovervilles" after President Hoover—cropped up at the edges of towns and cities. Getting almost no government help from the Hoover administration, charities in some cities and towns set up programs to attempt to feed the growing number of hungry and homeless people.

Many segments of society faced prejudice during the Great Depression. African Americans had faced heavy discrimination throughout the country long before the depression began. As the depression grew worse, working African Americans were often laid off from their jobs so that those jobs could be given to white workers. About 50 percent of African American workers were unemployed by 1932, significantly more than whites. Other minority groups faced similar pressure. Mexican Americans living in large cities like Detroit, Michigan, or in agricultural communities like California's San Joaquin Valley were sometimes seen as holding jobs that should go to whites. Programs were set up to persuade Mexican Americans to return to Mexico. Those who resisted were often threatened, intimidated, or beaten.

Many Mexican field workers lived in slums like these during the Great Depression. Minorities were seen by some as taking work that could go to white workers, even though they hardly had roofs over their heads.

Poor whites also faced discrimination. Farmers who lost their land to foreclosure or who fled drought conditions during the Dust Bowl years were forced to wander in search of work. Many went to West Coast states like California or Oregon in search of agricultural work. Those that found work were often badly paid and poorly treated.

CHAPTER 5
Recovering From a Depression

America survived the Great Depression even when many citizens didn't believe that was possible. America's experience with depressions proves it's possible to come out a depression, turn an economy around, and experience renewed growth. Coming out relies on multiple strategies. There is no single formula that will work in each new downturn. Different events spur depressions, and each depression is unique to the economy and times in which it occurs.

Programs for Relief and Policy Strategies

One important step in helping the economy recover is to set relief programs in place to help those in need. Relief programs may be relatively simple programs that distribute food or clothing to people in need. They may also be complex employment programs designed to find jobs for people who need work.

To bring the economy out of a slump, the government often makes policy changes designed to help businesses increase productivity and hire workers. The Federal Reserve System, which serves as a central bank, often lowers interest rates during a slump. The lower interest rates encourage borrowing and make it easier for individuals and businesses to repay lenders.

President Hoover and Congress raised taxes during the Great Depression, a move that many economists today feel made the crisis worse. The usual government response during economic slowdowns is to lower taxes. Lowering taxes lessens the tax burden on people and businesses. Money that they would ordinarily have spent on taxes can then be spent in other ways. Consumers can buy products, while businesses can increase production. This spending stimulates the economy and helps it climb out of the trough.

The government also uses tax refunds as another tool to encourage spending. With refunds, taxpayers are given a check from the Internal Revenue Service for a fixed amount. When the housing bubble burst in 2007, the government responded by issuing tax refunds to everyone who filled out

In 2008 President George W. Bush urged the US Congress to vote to pass a bailout package that he hoped would pull the struggling country out of financial crisis.

tax forms for the year 2007. Even people who did not have to pay any taxes for the year could receive a refund so long as they filled out the form.

To keep people employed during an economic slump, the government may also bail out struggling businesses that employ large numbers of workers. These bailouts, often used for large manufacturers like automakers, can come in the form of loans, grants, subsidies, or even management help. During the Great Depression, Herbert Hoover bailed out some investors. Similar action was taken in the fall of 2008, as the government approved a $700 billion package to help banks recover from bad mortgage loans.

Wars can help bring on depressions, just as the War of 1812 helped lead to the Panic of 1819. War reduces the number of workers available and often diverts production from retail goods to military supplies. When a war ends, economies may sink into recessions because there aren't enough job openings for the many thousands of soldiers returning to civilian life. The country may have spent vast sums of money on the war and now has to deal with serious debt. Factories and fields may have been wrecked by fighting, and large segments of the workforce may have died in fighting or fled to safety in other countries.

Ironically, war can also help bring a country out of a depression. The United States had come through the worst of the Great Depression by 1935, despite the recession of 1937. However, unemployment remained relatively high and production low until the United States became involved in World War II (1941–1945). Production leaped to all-time highs and unemployment dropped as factories went to work manufacturing supplies for the war effort. The economy continued to boom even after the war, as factories switched back from manufacturing military supplies to making consumer goods.

Depression Mentality

The years of hardship made a profound, even traumatic, impression on many Americans who lived through the Great Depression. Some had seen their homes taken away. Others had taken any work they could find, no matter how backbreaking, to put food on the table. Their experiences gave rise to an attitude toward money sometimes called a depression mentality.

Following a depression, survivors might have heightened worries about their financial future and save as much money as they can.

This mind-set is marked by extreme caution with spending and high concern about financial security. Many people who lived through the Great Depression were ever afterward frugal (low spending), unwilling to take on debt, and careful to save money for the future and in case of emergencies. During economic boom times, a depression mentality can seem overly cautious amid prosperity and bountiful financial opportunities. When the economy falters, however, people rediscover the importance of saving money and the wisdom of handling it safely and responsibly.

The New Deal and New Hope

President Franklin Roosevelt faced a daunting task when he took office in 1933. The nation's economy was in ruins. People across the country were disheartened. During his inauguration speech, Roosevelt sought to reassure the country by announcing that "the only thing we have to fear is fear itself."

Roosevelt immediately set to work to reassure the nation by beginning work on the New Deal. The massive New Deal program was a series of federal programs and agencies designed to counteract the effects of the depression. One of the goals of the New Deal was to lower production of crops and products to meet the low demand of consumers. Another goal was to increase consumer demand in part by supplying jobs for people in public works fields and getting cash back into their hands. With people earning money by building roads, dams, and schools, they once again had money to spend on goods and services.

One of Roosevelt's first actions was to get Congress to pass a nationwide bank holiday. On this day, all the country's banks would be closed and people would not be able to withdraw money. Congress also passed the Emergency Banking Act, a law calling for the government to inspect banks. Another law called the Glass-Steagall Act set tougher rules for banks. It also provided insurance to depositors through a new agency called the Federal Deposit Insurance Corporation (FDIC). Even today, this agency guarantees that people will not lose all of their money in the event of a bank collapse.

Other programs provided direct assistance to people in need. Several bills were passed to help farmers and homeowners pay their mortgages. The Federal Emergency Relief Agency provided grants to states that helped more than twenty million people through public works projects that gave them jobs and improved the quality of their lives. The Fair Standards of Labor Act limited the number of hours that most laborers could work and set the country's first minimum wage. The Social Security Act of 1935 included three major programs: a fund for retired workers, unemployment insurance for people who lose their jobs, and welfare grants for the poor.

Broader New Deal efforts included the Agricultural Adjustment Act, a law designed to raise farm prices. The National Industrial Recovery Act provided for an expanded national public works effort overseen by the Public Works Administration. It also included new guidelines to guarantee fair and competitive business practices.

While the New Deal did not end the Great Depression, it greatly lessened its severity. More people had jobs, and federal programs were put into place to help those unable to work. The New Deal programs also helped set up important government controls over the economy that helped the country better weather later recessions.

CHAPTER 6

Is Another Depression Likely?

The economy enjoyed a three-year growth spurt from 2003 to 2006. Rapid growth was fueled by low interest rates and easy access to credit. High-risk lending practices were common, especially in the housing market. Home prices rose rapidly as new home construction soared. It was the perfect storm for a downturn in the environment.

From 2003 to 2006, some sectors of the US economy grew rapidly. Low interest rates and high-risk lending practices made it easy for people to borrow money. The housing market, in particular, soared as home prices rose and people kept building new houses.

However, the economy began slowing in late 2006. Home sales dropped and so did new home construction. People who had built the new homes and businesses that had supplied building materials soon found that they had much less work than before. Despite the slump, the stock market kept rising, hitting an all-time high that year.

Yet, even the markets eventually dropped as bad news started coming in. Creditors lost money as people defaulted on their loans. In August 2008, unemployment rose to a five-year high of 6.1 percent, and credit tightened again. Some banks were even taken to the brink of collapse and were bought out by other banks. The government took steps to bail out mortgage lenders Fannie Mae and Freddie Mac, as well as insurance giant AIG. In September 2008, the government even passed a $700 billion rescue plan to help struggling banks.

Mixed Bag of Blame and Hope

In the fall of 2008, many economists predicted that the economy could fall into a severe recession or even a depression. Some economists felt the regulations that were put in place during the Great Depression had been seriously weakened over time and, as a result, the FDIC might not be able to guarantee deposits in the event of a full-scale banking collapse. They pointed out that deregulating the activities of banks and lenders had brought on the credit crises by undoing some of these economic controls.

Other economists dismissed the idea. During the Great Depression, new policies were put into action governing the way that banks do business and guaranteeing that money held by the banks would be insured. Economists felt that these safeguards—along with a broader government relief system than any that existed when the Great Depression began—would protect the economy in this latest crisis. Unlike when Herbert Hoover was in office, the government now willingly spends itself into a deficit to spur the economy and protect its citizens. Also, governments today are more ready to step in and offer direct aid to individuals and businesses during an economic crisis. In fact, in late 2008, President-elect Barack Obama proposed an economic stimulus and rescue package that involved public works projects, homeowner and taxpayer relief, and assistance to banks, manufacturers, and small businesses. The cost of this large and ambitious plan was estimated

ECONOMIC DEPRESSION

Weather: Sunny, 75/52 — **SPORTS ★ FINAL** — **Thursday, September 18, 2008**

DAILY◉NEWS

50¢ **2.5 MILLION READERS EVERY DAY** NYDailyNews.com

Why Jeter is Yankee fans' champion
MIKE LUPICA ON DEREK'S 1,000TH GAME AT THE STADIUM — SEE PAGE 3

Amazin's hold off Nationals, 9-7
FULL COVERAGE SEE SPORTS

THE BAIL FAILS

CRISIS ON WALL STREET

- Dow falls 449 despite fed rescue of insurance giant
- Growing fear that more agony in store for big firms

COMPLETE COVERAGE ON PAGES 4-6

In 2006 the economy's rapid growth slowed significantly, and even a government bailout in 2008 couldn't save the country from the stubborn slump.

to be as much as one trillion dollars. In February 2009, President Obama signed this package into law.

Similarities

There are some similarities, however, in the circumstances that caused the Great Depression and the financial crisis of 2008. Banks and lending institutions, including some very old and respected firms, went under (failed) in 2008, just as they did in 1929. Unemployment rose dramatically and spending fell sharply in both eras. In both economic crises, the stock market fell dramatically and stocks lost much of their value. Yet, these same kinds of events have occurred in several recessions since the Great Depression.

Just as in 1929, in 2008 major banks and businesses failed and were forced to close their doors.

During those recessions, economists would sometimes issue dire warnings of coming depressions. Instead, the economy recovered after a period of months or even years. While conditions were bad during these times, they never resulted in a depression.

Given the effective protections and safeguards put into the economy during the Great Depression, chances are good that the economic crisis of 2008 will be viewed in future years as a strong and serious recession, but one that the nation actively pulled itself out of, thereby avoiding another depression.

CHAPTER 7

A Relative Calm

Seven years after the Great Recession, the panic-stricken atmosphere of the economic crises of 2008 no longer existed. By the close of the second quarter of 2015, job growth had hit a new high. The unemployment rate rose a bit, however, as demand for jobs outpaced supply. In the housing market, foreclosures were down. New home construction also increased, an important indicator that homebuilders expected consumers to have money needed to purchase new homes.

In the relative calm, the Federal Reserve Board moved closer to its goal of raising an important interest rate, a hike expected by September if economic indicators continued to show that making that policymaking decision would help the economy. The economy's health determines how the Fed advances its policies.

Assessing a Healthy Economy

Let's return to a comparison discussed earlier in this resource. The doctor's approach to his or her patient's health is quite similar to the economist's approach to the health of the economy. Doctors ask patients about who, what, when, where, why, and how pain, illness or physical discomfort occurred. They want to figure out the source of the problem to properly assess and treat it. The economist assesses the economy is essentially the same way, analyzing the source of the problem in order to begin to figure out how to best move forward and toward a healthy economy.

Finding Jobs Today

Technology is changing how workers find jobs. In today's digital hiring marketplace, many employees use company websites to begin the recruitment process. Some items found on company websites include job listings and electronic applications. Questionnaires are other common tools located online. Those test trustworthiness, reliability, punctuality, and other favorable job qualities.

Don't waste time by first visiting retail stores, fast food restaurants, or other local employers who hire part-time and seasonal workers. Rather, visit the related websites of your preferred employers. Find desirable jobs and locations. Then, complete applications and either follow up onsite or wait to be contacted, depending on the automatic response generated from your search efforts.

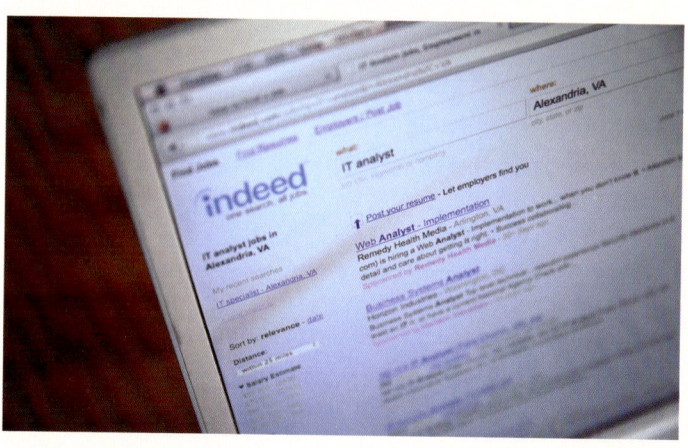

With the quick click of a mouse and a few swift keystrokes, you can check out local and worldwide job openings listed online, all from the comfort of your own computer.

In spring 2015, hopeful traders on the New York Stock Exchange watched as stocks rose and the thought of a healthy, thriving economy looked possible.

In the back and forth—ebb and flow—of the business cycle the economy is always analyzed for its overall health. Is it strong? Are there signs of sluggishness? Is any area showing signs of weakness? Is it stressed? Will it recover? Like doctors assessing patient health, economists watch the economy for signs of general well-being. They draw conclusions based on observations from what is seen, heard, and experienced by Americans across the country. They ask pointed inquiries, honing in the "5 W's and H"—who, what, when, where, why and how. During a recession the pointed questions include many of the following:

- **Who is affected?** The answer provides a clearer picture of the scope of the depression. It goes beyond individuals to include industries, cities, and states.

- **What are the "symptoms"?** Visible signs of a downturn may include price fluctuations, bank failures, high unemployment, or a sharp decline in the stock market.

- **When did it begin?** Economists may have to backtrack months before the economic "symptoms" appeared to determine the actual time frame for the depression's start.

- **Where is it?** Economists determine if the situation is limited to one area of the country or rippling around the nation.

- **Why did it happen?** Various factors impact the business cycle. One possible why: an economic "shock" such as a natural disaster spiraled into a much larger economic crisis.

- **How can it be turned around?** If there is a way to stop or curtail the depression, economists want to know how to do so.

Questions abounded at the end of the second quarter although the economy appeared healthy and strong. How long that remains depends on the business cycle and its usual movements to keep the economy at a level where America can be a productive nation and global citizen.

Focus Forward

The economy's ever-changing nature makes it impossible to determine if America will ever experience another devastating downturn like the Great Depression. Many agree that the country came close during 2007–2009. For reasons discussed in this book, America avoided another depression, enabling the country to bounce back quicker than some anticipated. However, lessons learned during that crises remain fresh in the hearts and minds of

Americans, especially for those still feeling the sting of underemployment or housing instability.

Is there hope for the economy? When you consider that economic downturns are part of the business cycle, the answer is yes. Remember, change is inevitable! At some point, a downturn in the economy *eventually* shifts due to policy changes or other factors. The economy picks up and the country experiences improvements in many—if not all—sectors of the economy. It is possible that America will not experience a depression during your lifetime. Then again, it might. Nonetheless, understanding what an economic depression is and how it works inspires a hopeful, resilient outlook. While depressions may occur, history proves they do not last forever. Knowing this makes it potentially easier to weather any economic climate.

Timeline of the History of US Depressions

1819 The Panic of 1819 spurs the first depression.

1837 The Panic of 1837 is caused by collapsed cotton prices and failed wheat crops, among other factors.

1857 The Panic of 1857 is triggered by the collapse of the Ohio Life Insurance and Trust Company.

1873 The Panic of 1873 is set off by railroad speculation.

1893 The Panic of 1893 is the last nineteenth-century depression.

October 24, 1929 On "Black Tuesday" the stock market crashes, representing the start of the Great Depression.

1930 By March, the number of workers out of work reaches 3.2 million, more than double the number before Black Tuesday.

1930–1936 Severe drought strikes parts of Midwestern and Great Plains states.

1931 The Bank of the United States, the fourth largest New York City bank, fails in December; by end of Great Depression nearly five thousand banks had failed.

1932 "Hoovervilles" crop up at edges of cities and towns; Reconstruction Finance Corporation is established by Congress in January to lend money to failing banks and other companies.

1933 Franklin D. Roosevelt is elected president and begins "New Deal" efforts; Glass-Steagall Act establishes the Federal Deposit Insurance Company, which guarantees bank deposits up to a certain amount.

1935 Social Security Act becomes law.

1936, 1940 Franklin D. Roosevelt wins reelection for second and third terms.

1941–1945 American's involvement in World War II results in increased production, lower unemployment, and other economic benefits, leading to the end of the Great Depression.

Bibliographic Sources

Acton, Johnny. *Eyewitness Economy*. New York, NY: D.K., 2010.

Bonner, Bill, and Addison Wiggin. *Empire of Debt: The Rise of an Epic Financial Crisis*. Hoboken, NJ: John Wiley & Sons, Inc., 2006.

Bush, George W. "President Bush's Speech to the Nation on the Economic Crisis." *New York Times*, September 24, 2008. Retrieved June 2015 (http://www.nytimes.com/2008/09/24/business/economy/24text-bush.html?_r=0&pagewanted=print).

Cameron, Rondo. *A Concise Economic History of the World: From Paleolithic Times to the Present*. 3rd ed. New York, NY: Oxford University Press, 1997.

Fleming, Sam. "No Spring Bounce in Flat US Economy." *Financial Times*, May 15, 2015. Retrieved June 2015 (http://www.ft.com/intl/cms/s/0/2f3de8ce-fb18-11e4-9aed-00144feab7de.html#axzz3e3SJgw7Y).

Flynn, Sean Masaki. *Economics for Dummies*. Hoboken, NJ: Wiley, 2011.

Galbraith, John Kenneth. *The Great Crash: 1929*. Boston, Mass.: Houghton Mifflin Company, 1988.

Gordon, John Steele. *An Empire of Wealth: The Epic History of American Economic Power*. New York, NY: HarperCollins Publishers, 2004.

Gottheil, Fred. *Principles of Economics*. 4th ed. Mason, OH: Thomson Publishing, 2005.

Heinrichs, Ann. *The Great Recession*. New York, NY: Nomad Press, 2014.

Krugman, Paul. *The Return of Depression Economics*. New York, NY: W. W. Norton & Company, 1999.

Lange, Brenda. *The Stock Market Crash of 1929: The End of Prosperity*. New York, NY: Chelsea House, 2007.

Lanigan, Jane, ed. *Economics: Economic History*. Vol. 6. Danbury, Conn.: Grolier Educational, 2000.

Lanigan, Jane, ed. *Economics: Economic Theory*. Vol. 5. Danbury, Conn.: Grolier Educational, 2000.

Lawson, Alan. *A Commonwealth of Hope: The New Deal Response to Crisis*. Baltimore, MD: The Johns Hopkins University Press, 2006.

Lowenstein, Roger. *Origins of the Crash: The Great Bubble and Its Undoing*. New York, NY: The Penguin Press, 2004.

McElvaine, Robert S. *The Great Depression: America, 1929–1941*. New York, NY: Times Books, 1993.

Mian, Atif and Amir Sufi. *House of Debt: How They (and You) Caused the Great Recession, and How We Can Prevent It From Happening Again*. Chicago, Ill.: The University of Chicago Press, 2014.

Nardo, Don, ed. *The Great Depression*. San Diego, CA: Greenhaven Press, Inc., 2000.

Puzzanghera, Jim. "Economy Has Recovered 8.7 Million Jobs Lost in Great Recession." *Los Angeles Times*, June 6, 2014. Retrieved June 2015 (http://www.latimes.com/business/la-fi-jobs-20140607-story.html).

Rauchway, Eric. *The Great Depression and the New Deal: A Very Short Introduction*. New York, NY: Oxford University Press, 2008.

San Diego Zoo. "*Birds. Ostrich*," San Diego Zoo. Retrieved June 2015 (http://animals.sandiegozoo.org/animals/ostrich).

Sowell, Thomas. *Basic Economics: A Citizen's Guide to the Economy*. New York, NY: Basic Books, 2000.

Sparshott, Jeffrey. "Economists React to the May Jobs Report: 'Unambiguously Positive.'" *The Wall Street Journal*, June 5, 2015. Retrieved June 2015 (http://blogs.wsj.com/economics/2015/06/05/economists-react-to-the-may-jobs-report-unambiguously-positive/?KEYWORDS=Sparshott+jobs).

Steeples, Douglas, and David O. Whitten. *Democracy in Desperation: The Depression of 1893*. Westport, Conn.: Greenwood Press, 1998.

Temin, Peter. "The Great Recession and the Great Depression." NBER Working Paper No. 15645, January 2010. Retrieved June 2015 (http://www.nber.org/papers/w15645).

US Department of State. "Smoot-Hawley Tariff." US Department of State. Retrieved October 27, 2015 (http://future.state.gov/when/timeline/1921_timeline/smoot_tariff.html).

Von Hoffman, Constantine. "Report: Economy Will Be Flat Until 2015." CBS News, MoneyWatch, July 22, 2013. Retrieved June 2015 (http://www.cbsnews.com/news/report-economy-will-be-flat-until-2015/).

Glossary

bankruptcy—A legal process intended to ensure equality among the creditors of a corporation or individual declared to be bankrupt, or a person or corporation's inability to discharge all debts as they come due.

bond—A certificate of ownership of a specified portion of a debt due to be paid by a government or corporation to an individual holder and usually bearing a fixed rate of interest.

business cycle—A term describing how the economy functions, either up (expansion) or down (contraction).

corporation—An organized body, especially a business, that has been granted a state charter recognizing it as a separate legal entity having its own rights, privileges, and liabilities distinct from those of the individuals within the entity.

credit—Confidence in a purchaser's ability and intention to pay, displayed by entrusting the buyer with goods or services without immediate payment.

currency—Something that is used as a medium of exchange; money.

debt—Something that is owed or that one is bound to pay to or perform for another.

deficit—The amount by which costs or debts exceed income or assets.

deflation—A fall in the general price level or a contraction of credit and available money.

depression—A period during which business, employment, and stock market values decline severely or remain at a very low level of activity.

economy—A network of producers, distributors, and consumers of goods and services in a local, regional, national, or global community.

foreclosure—A legal process where the bank takes back a home when a homeowner cannot pay the mortgage loan.

Great Recession—The economic downturn in the United States from December 2007 to June 2009.

gross domestic product (GDP)—The total market value of goods and services produced by workers and capital within a nation's borders during a given period.

gross national product (GNP)—The total monetary value of all final goods and services produced in a country during one year.

interest—A sum paid or charged for the use of money or for borrowing money, often expressed as a percentage of money borrowed and to be paid back within a given time.

production—The process of producing goods that have exchange value.

profit—The monetary surplus left to a producer or employer after deducting wages, rent, cost of raw materials, etc.

recession—A period of general economic decline, defined usually as a contraction in the GDP for six months or longer. Marked by high unemployment, stagnant wages, and falling retail sales, a recession generally does not last longer than one year and is much milder than a depression.

speculation—The putting together of an idea or theory without any concrete facts or evidence.

stagnate—To stop developing or moving; to cease action.

stock—Ownership shares of a particular company or corporation.

tariff—A government tax on imports or exports.

Further Reading

Books

Donovan, Sandra. *Budgeting Smarts: How to Set Goals, Save Money, Spend Wisely, and More.* Minneapolis, Minn.: Twenty-First Century Books, 2012.

Duignan, Brian (Editor). *The Great Depression (Economics: Taking the Mystery Out of Money).* New York, NY: Rosen Education Service, 2013.

Heinrichs, Ann. *The Great Recession.* New York, NY: Scholastic Inc., 2012.

Koss, Amy Goldman. *The Not-So-Great Depression: In Which the Economy Crashes, My Sister's Plans Are Ruined, My Mom Goes Broke, My Dad Grows Vegetables, and I Do Not Get a Hamster.* New York, NY: Roaring Brook Press, 2010.

Lusted, Marcia Amidon. *The Roaring Twenties: Discover the Era of Prohibition, Flappers, and Jazz (Inquire and Investigate).* White River Junction, VT: Nomad Press, 2014.

Porterfield, Jason. *How a Recession Affects You.* New York, NY: Rosen Publishing Group, 2013.

Sylvester, Kevin. *Follow Your Money: Who Gets It, Who Spends It, Where Does It Go?* Toronto, Canada: Annick Press, 2013.

Watkins, Heidi, Book Editor. *Consumer Culture.* Farmington Hills, Mich.: Greenhaven Press, 2011.

Websites

The Federal Reserve and the Financial Crisis: Interactive Timeline
www.federalreserve.gov/aboutthefed/cls-timeline/timeline/
An interactive financial crisis timeline.

Franklin D. Roosevelt Presidential Library and Museum
www.fdrlibrary.marist.edu/index.html
Virtual tour, information, and resources about America's first presidential library.

Great Depression
www.history.com/topics/great-depression
The History Channel's guide to the Great Depression.

Library of Congress. "Great Depression for Students"
www.loc.gov/teachers/classroommaterials/themes/great-depression/students.html
Resources and activities from the Library of Congress.

President Bush's Speech to the Nation on the Economic Crisis
www.nytimes.com/2008/09/24/business/economy/24text-bush.html?_r=0&pagewanted=print
Transcript of Former President George W. Bush's speech to the nation.

Riding the Rails
www.pbs.org/wgbh/americanexperience/films/rails/
Film about teens' experiences riding freight trains during the Great Depression.

The New Deal Network
newdeal.feri.org/index.htm
Check out this educational tool about the Great Depression and its effects on many areas of society.

Index

A
Agricultural Adjustment Act, 69
AIG, 71

B
bank failures, 26, 32, 41–42, 78
bank holiday, 68
bankruptcy, 14, 52–53,
Black Thursday, 31
British pound, 41
booms, 11, 20, 29–31, 38, 66, 67
bubbles, 11, 21, 65–66
Bush, President George W., 7

C
consumer price index, 48
cotton prices (as an indicator of economic health), 21
credit, 14, 15, 21, 26, 31, 32, 37, 54, 70, 71
creditors, 52–54, 70
crime, 58

D
deficit, 46, 71
deflation, 42
depression mentality, 67
depressions,
    causes of, 27–29
    definition of, 7
    early examples of, 20–24
    effects of, 14, 37, 50–58
    explanation of, 11–13, 14
    history of the term, 15
    myths and facts, 36
    recovery from, 14, 64–66

Detroit, Michigan, 61
Dillinger, John, 58
Dust Bowl, 44, 63
Dust Bowl Ballads, 44

E
e-commerce, 55
economic indicators, 15–16, 19, 37, 75
economy stages/phases of, 11
Emergency Banking Act, 68
employment/unemployment rate, 15, 50–52

F
Fair Standards of Labor Act, 69
Fannie Mae, 71
Federal Deposit Insurance Corporation (FDIC), 68, 71
Federal Emergency Relief Agency, 68
Federal Reserve, 42, 64, 75,
Federal Reserve System, 64
financial crisis of 2008, 70–74
foreclosures, 7, 58, 63, 75
Freddie Mac, 71

G
Glass-Steagall Act, 68
globalization, 11
gold reserves, 42
gold standard, 41–42
government bailouts, 14, 66, 71
Grapes of Wrath, The, 44
Great Britain, 21, 41–42
Great Depression
    beginning of, 29–31

deepening of, 32–35, 38–40, 46, 47
effect on minority groups, 61
end of, 69
government response to, 38, 48, 65, 68–69
life during, 56–58, 58–63, 67
Great Recession, 7, 75
gross domestic product (GDP), 16, 19
gross national product (GNP), 16, 19
Guthrie, Woody, 44

H
Hoover, President Herbert, 31–32, 38–40, 46–47, 56–58, 61, 65–66, 71
"Hoovervilles," 61

I
inflation, 11, 15, 22, 27–29
interest rate, lowering of, 14, 64, 70
interest rate, raising of, 42, 75

J
Jay Cooke and Company, 23
June 28, 1932 riot, 59
June 1932 march on Washington, 59

L
land speculation, 21

M
Mexico, 61
monopolies, effect on economy, 31

N
National Industrial Recovery Act, 69
natural disasters, effect on the economy of, 29, 78
New Deal, 48, 68–69

O
Obama, Barack, 8, 71–73
October 24, 1929, 31
Ohio Life Insurance and Trust Company, 22–23

P
Panic of 1819, 21, 66
Panic of 1837, 21–22
Panic of 1857, 21, 22–23
Panic of 1873, 21, 23
Panic of 1893, 21, 24
Parker, Bonnie, and Clyde Barrow, 58
peaks (as part of an economic cycle), 19–20, 52
President's Committee for Employment, 38
price fluctuations, effect on the economy of, 27–28, 78
Public Works Administration, 69

R
railroad speculation, 23
recessions, explanation of, 11, 13–14, 15, 19–20
recovery (as part of an economic cycle), 19–20
relief programs, 64–66
Republican Party, 56–58
Roosevelt, Franklin Delano, 48, 58, 68
"run on the bank," 32

S
San Joaquin Valley, California, 61
Smoot-Hawley Tariff, 47
Social Security Act, 69
Steinbeck, John, 44
stock market, 11, 14, 21, 23, 26, 31, 35, 36, 47, 54, 70, 73, 78

T
tariffs, 46–47
tax rebates, 14
tax refunds, 65–66
trough (as part of an economic cycle), 19–20, 65

W
War of 1812, 21, 66
wars, effect on economy, 21, 29, 46, 66
World War I, 29, 31, 46, 59, 66
World War II, 66

WITHDRAWN

22.84   7/14/16.

LONGWOOD PUBLIC LIBRARY
800 Middle Country Road
Middle Island, NY 11953
(631) 924-6400
mylpl.net

LIBRARY HOURS

Monday-Friday	9:30 a.m. - 9:00 p.m.
Saturday	9:30 a.m. - 5:00 p.m.
Sunday (Sept-June)	1:00 p.m. - 5:00 p.m.